GROW DOWN

HOW TO BUILD
A JESUS-CENTERED FAITH

simply for students

KEN CASTOR

YouthMinistry.com/TOGETHER

Grow Down
How to Build a Jesus-Centered Faith

© 2014 Ken Castor

group.com

simplyyouthministry.com

Credits
Author: Ken Castor
Executive Developer: Jason Ostrander
Chief Creative Officer: Joani Schultz
Editor: Rob Cunningham
Copy Editor: Stephanie Martin
Art Director: Veronica Preston
Production Artist: Brian Fuglestad

ISBN 978-1-4707-1354-6

10 9 8 7 6 5 4 3 2   20 19 18 17 16 15 14

Printed in the United States of America.

DEDICATION

Kathy, Zach, Ben, and Elly:
Thank you for growing down with me.

In celebration of Galen Dolby.

5/1/15

JAMES
CONGRATS!
MAY YOU ALWAYS GO DEEPER
w/ JESUS -
- Ken Gretor
col 2:6-7

ACKNOWLEDGEMENTS

To all those in Canada, the U.S., and Northern Ireland who have borne my immaturity over the years and who have helped shape the idea of this book, thank you for partnering with me in strong, fruitful ministry. To Kathy, Zach, Ben, and Elly for contributing amazing ideas and for encouraging me daily. To my colleagues and students at Crown College, to my fellow youth workers in the Christian & Missionary Alliance, and to my dear friends at Brentview in Calgary and at Youth for Christ in Northern Ireland: Thank you for engaging with me and my countless, poorly drawn "tree diagrams." To Steven McCready, Dan Leffelaar, Wilbur Sargunaraj, Gary Newton, Jason Ostrander, Matt Reeve, Brittany Nelson, Ginny Olson, Brad Mock, and Matty McCage: Thank you for your listening ear, creative vision, and personal enrichment of this simple message. Thanks to Stephanie Krajec, Rob Cunningham, Rick Lawrence, and the amazing team at Group for moving this project toward print.

TABLE OF CONTENTS

Introduction VII

PART I: THE PROBLEM WITH GROWING UP

Chapter 1: Warning: Adult Content! 1

Chapter 2: Three Habits of an Adulterated Faith 11

Chapter 3: You're Growing the Wrong Way! 23

PART II: GROW DOWN

Chapter 4: Greatest in the Kingdom 33

Chapter 5: Rooted in Christ 43

Chapter 6: Unlimited Growth &
               Unlimited Resources 59

PART III: DRAW UP

Chapter 7: Standing Strong in the Truth 69

Chapter 8: Withstanding Winds 77

Chapter 9: Scars That Become Beauty Marks 85

PART IV: GO OUT

Chapter 10: If You Can Contain Jesus… 97

Chapter 11: The Overflowing Life 107

Chapter 12: Seeing the Forest 119

Conclusion: Rooted Faith 129

Endnotes 133

INTRODUCTION

If "up" is the direction you are growing, stop now!

The pages that follow contain a radical pattern that runs counter to contemporary ideas about adulthood. It's the oldest and truest pattern. Imagine a tree—where life is rooted, standing strong, and overflowing with life.

So rather than trying to grow up, this book encourages you to grow down into Jesus, and then to draw up from his unlimited resources and go out with an abundance of life that this world desperately needs.

That's what a Jesus-centered life looks like.

HOW TO USE THIS BOOK

Interact! Draw pictures, brainstorm your thoughts, and spread your ideas with the hashtag #growdown. Star your favorite phrases and scribble your best notes all over the pages that follow. Each chapter contains questions and activities meant to stir your reflection. You can go through this book on your own or explore it through a series of discussions with a small group of friends.

However you use it, may this book help you root into a deeper discovery of true life.

Grow Down,

– Ken Castor

*And now, just as you accepted Christ Jesus as Lord, you must continue to live in obedience to him. Let your roots **grow down** into Christ…and **draw up** nourishment from him, so that you will grow in faith, strong and vigorous in the truth you were taught. Let your lives **overflow** with thanksgiving for all he has done.*

– Colossians 2:6-7 (NLT 1996, bold added)

PART I:
THE PROBLEM WITH GROWING UP

"Adult: A person who has stopped growing at both ends
and is now growing in the middle."

– Urban Dictionary[1]

CHAPTER 1
WARNING: ADULT CONTENT!

GROW
DOWN

Among the greatest achievements of the grown*up* world is the creation of the Twinkie®, a yellowish cake-like dessert with a cream-like filling loaded with sugars and flavoring and glue-like chemicals.[2] Twinkies have been described as the "icon of junk food snacks and guilty pleasures, nutritionally worthless yet irresistibly yummy." Legend says that Twinkies could survive both a store shelf for 30 years and a nuclear attack.[3]

But you shouldn't begin hoarding Twinkies in preparation for that nuclear zombie apocalypse. Tests have shown that after 30 years, Twinkies actually will chemically break down and, sadly, they'd be no match against a nuclear bomb.

Adults are a lot like Twinkies.

In order to look good and be filled, adults add a lot of guilty pleasures to their lives. But by the age of 30, even though they are slow to admit it, adults show signs of chemically breaking down. And against a nuclear attack, an adult doesn't stand much of a chance.

WHAT DO YOU WANT TO BE?

When you were younger, somebody probably asked you one of life's little questions: "What do you want to be when you grow *up*?" (People may *still* ask you that question!) While your answer might have been great for you at that time (such as a firefighter, a racecar driver, or a rock star), the question misguides the purpose of your life.

- First of all, what you are doing right now is just as important to God as what you will be doing in the future.

- Second of all, growing *up* is not as great as we've been made to think. It makes us think that adding more stuff is the best way to gain freedom. It tricks us into thinking that selfishness is the key to friendships. And as you might have noticed in the questionable behavior of some adults you know, it doesn't even guarantee maturity.

The word *adult* is made up of two Latin words: *ad,* which means "toward" or "add,"[4] and *ultus,* which means "fully grown." At least grammatically speaking, an adult is someone who has "added enough to their life to have fully grown." The first two dictionary definitions of the word *adult* reflect this:[5]

> **a·dult** [uh-**duhlt**, **ad**-uhlt] 1: fully developed and mature: grown-up / **2:** of, relating to, intended for, or befitting adults <an ***adult*** approach to a problem>

Grown*ups* sit at the *adult* table during family meals because they are oozing with fully developed maturity, right? If this is true, then why does the third definition of *adult* in the dictionary take such a disturbing turn?

> **a·dult 3**: dealing in or with explicitly sexual material <***adult*** bookstores> <***adult*** movies>

The word *adult* is filled with questionable ingredients. Does this math equation look correct to you: Grown*up* + Explicit Sex = Adult? I don't blame the dictionary for describing what "we" mean by our language. But by what form of grammatical gymnastics does the combination of these things make sense?

Virtually everyone in our messed-up-and-confused-morals culture understands that exposing children to that sort of thing is inherently wrong.[6] Yet at some point, as a person grows *up*, our society believes and even expects explicit behavior. Even if it diminishes dignity, ruins innocence, creates addictions, and damages relationships, adults feel justified to add explicit things to their supposedly "developed" lives. Like a spider entrapping a victim in its web, *adulthood* seduces people into a deceptive trap.

Maybe the following definition is much more befitting of many adults:

> **child·ish** [**chahyl**-dish]: marked by or suggestive of immaturity and lack of poise
> <a ***childish*** spiteful remark>[7]

Growing *up* doesn't stop people from childishness; it just gives them more experience at it. Most grownups have moments of melting down, dissing someone, spreading gossip, becoming more stubborn ("You can't make me!"), making senseless decisions, and throwing tantrums.

A HOT DOG MADE OF HORSE LIPS?

As if the problems with the word *adult* weren't substantial enough, if *ad* is combined with another prefix, *alter* (which means "other"),[8] other truly sinister grown*up* words are generated:

> **a·dul·ter·ate** [*uh*-**duhl**-*tuh*-reyt]: to corrupt, debase, or make impure by the addition of a foreign or inferior substance or element.[9]

You'd be pretty ticked (or feel pretty pukey) if you bought a hot dog that was advertised as "all beef" but turned out to be full of horse lips and chicken intestines. Someone adulterated that hot dog by adding junk that never should have been added. That's exactly what many people do with their lives when they grow *up*.

> **a·dul·ter·y** [*uh*-**duhl**-*tuh*-ree]: sex between a married person and someone who is not that person's wife or husband.[10]

There is a reason it's not called "childery." Children don't commit adultery. Adults commit adultery.[11] Yet our society pushes children toward that pattern. Adultery is the sad culmination of a twisted process of development that corrupts the heart of once-innocent people. Forty-five years ago, as he considered the self-absorption of North American adults, one philosopher concluded, "Today's child is growing up absurd!"[12] Since then, I fear, the situation has gotten worse.

Blame it on Adam and Eve, if you want. They began innocently enough in an unspoiled relationship with God. Then for some mind-blowing reason, they got swept up in temptation and added the knowledge of evil to their formerly blameless lives. I guess they felt that the fulfillment they had wasn't enough for them. They wanted more. They became dissatisfied, so they added another ingredient. They adulterated their lives—and grew *up* in a hurry.

RESISTING PANEM

In *The Hunger Games* series by Suzanne Collins, a society of adults living in a post-apocalyptic nation called Panem had become insatiably addicted to self-indulgence. Their explicit minds devised a contest where innocent children were pitted in battle to the death. The more flamboyant the drama and the more grotesque the violence, the more these adults salivated. The only hope for redemption rested in some simple, radical teenagers who had to learn to stand uncorrupted in a complicated, adult world.

In the landscape of our real world, the situation is just as dire. We need an uncorrupted generation to rise up from the adulterated ashes of our civilization. One of the last verses in the whole Bible, Revelation 21:27, tells us that nothing impure will enter the kingdom of heaven. From beginning to end, the Bible urges younger generations to resist the winds of this world and, instead, to grow in God's patterns.

Ultimately, we were created to have a pure relationship with God. "Faith is the gaze of a soul upon a saving God," wrote A.W. Tozer.[13] For a generation of self-absorbed adults, the call to a Jesus-centered life means there is no room for self-centeredness.

TILLING THE SOIL:

- How is an adult like a Twinkie?
  (Spread the word: #growdown)

- When you were younger, what did you want to be when you "grew *up*"? Why?

- In what ways have you personally noticed the pressure for young people to "grow *up*" in our society?

- Which of the key words surprised you the most in this chapter, and why?

- Why do you think people give in to the temptation to adulterate their lives?

- List three things you've added to your life that can mess up your love for God:

    1.

    2.

    3.

- How can you pray in response to this chapter?

CHAPTER 2:
THREE HABITS OF AN ADULTERATED FAITH

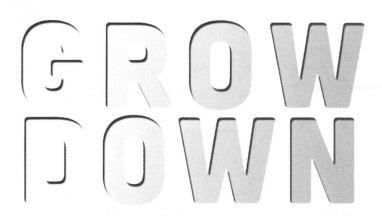

GROW DOWN

Statistics have shown that those who live the longest also happen to be the ones who have the most birthdays. (Go ahead; let that one sink in for a moment.) Personally, I seem to have about one birthday every year, which is identical to the international average. (Yeah, let that one sink in, too.) One of my most enjoyable birthdays was the year my parents gave me a 1-pound bag of gummy bears. Those hundreds of colorful, gelatinous, and allegedly digestible bears taught me that birthdays are amazing.

(1.)

(2)

God created birthdays for you. God created you, and he created time. And God created you to enjoy the time. As you age, you might get a little wrinkly. But who cares—that didn't stop Yoda, Methuselah, giant sea turtles, or redwood trees from being cool.

> *Quick: Name three things about Yoda, Methuselah, giant sea turtles, or redwood trees that are cool:*

1. Methuselah—lived longest in bible
   Yoda—
2. Known for legendary wisdom

3. sea turtles—born at 5cm long → grow to be 1.5 meters

So, you should grow *older.* redwood trees → first redwood came about dinosaurs time → oldest over 2000 years

But you shouldn't grow *up*.

Believing that the ultimate goal of life when we get older is to become a grown*up* is like thinking that eating an entire 1-pound bag of gummy bears on your birthday won't make you constipated. The problem is that it's often difficult to realize how something can plug up your true enjoyment of life until after you've digested it. Trust me on this one. Ugh…

③

As grown*ups* get older, they begin to hate birthdays. People wish they could be perpetually 29 years old, even after reaching their late 30s. Milestone years like 30, 40, or 50 can trigger deep psychological disturbances in the Force. Grown*ups* begin to long for the glory days of their childhood, when life was fun and they didn't feel stuck in their ways.

The disruption of our enjoyment of birthdays begins with three basic ideas that our society has about adulthood.[14] So if you show these three signs, supposedly, you're all grown *up*:

agree?

1. Independence

2. Self-dependence

3. Co-dependence

} is that true?

- "Independent" people think they have the power to make their own decisions and pursue their own desires. This sounds like a great thing when you're tired of your mom telling you to pick your clothes up off the floor.

- "Self-dependent" people think they have the power to stand on their own two feet. This sounds like a great thing when your dad embarrasses you by dropping you off at your friend's house and then continuing to wave at you from the driveway until you go in the front door.

- "Co-dependent" people think they are entitled to always feel good and to pursue things or relationships that make them feel affirmed, comfortable, or self-satisfied. This sounds like a great thing when you're bored or bummed.

Do those things define grown-up?
—not totally
why?

I Timothy 4:12

Each one, in its own right, is not necessarily horrible. And, in fact, there are some worthy aspects to each one. It's important to learn how to brush your teeth and do laundry and cook your own mac and cheese — and feel good about being able to do all of that. But the problem is that these three ideas, when stirred together, create a ridiculous recipe. Instead of providing satisfaction as we grow *up*, these ingredients actually cause three soul-clogging habits:

THREE BAD HABITS OF "ADULT" FAITH...

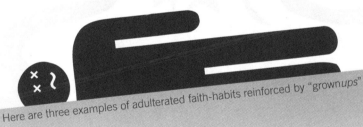

Here are three examples of adulterated faith-habits reinforced by "grown*ups*"

1. UNFAITHFULNESS

Independence entices people to follow other desires

(So students walk away from faith after high school)

MATTHEW 18:1–7

2. FALSE SECURITY

Self-dependence causes delusion

(So students lose their footing when pressures blow against them)

3. CHILDISHNESS

Co-dependence reinforces unhealthy relationships and selfish pursuits

(So students struggle to keep their childlike trust & faith)
1ˢᵗ Corinthians 13:11

1. INDEPENDENCE LEADS TO UNFAITHFULNESS

People were created for dependence upon God. So a stance in life that stresses "independence" entices people to pursue a path other than what God desires.

"To obey" simply means "to listen." Throughout the Bible, God tells everyone, "Listen!"[15] We know children need to obey, right? What about adults? Don't they need to obey, too?

But like a child cupping her hands over her ears and screaming, "I can't hear you!" independent people have ears but refuse to hear God.[16] Independence entices people toward disobedience, an un-listening attitude, and freedom from anyone else's control. In the end, it becomes more about defiance than freedom. That was Lucifer's downfall, by the way.[17] It's hard to be loyal to God when you won't listen to him.

adults do that to
- too hard? not enough energy?
pretend it isn't there

2. SELF–DEPENDENCE LEADS TO FALSE SECURITY

Have you ever gotten a ribbon for finishing last?

One of my sons got mad at me a few years ago when I made him go to his track meet on a cold drizzly day. To get back at me, he left his shoes untied. "Do you want me to help you tie your shoes?" I asked him. "I'm not going to tie my shoes ever again," he retorted, "so I won't ever need your help." When it was time for his 200-meter dash, he lined up with the four other runners. *"On the mark!"* But he didn't crouch into the starting position. *"Get set!"* He decided instead to just stand there and stare at me. *"Go!"* As the other runners took off racing down their lanes, my son started to walk—slowly, staring at me the whole way. When he finally stepped across the finish line, several frustratingly long minutes behind the other four runners, he was still glaring at me.

That's when some attendant ran up to him and gave him a ribbon for fifth place. "Way to go!" the volunteer said. "You did it!" I wanted to give that volunteer a piece of my mind.

- Did he deserve it?

- Should everyone get a ribbon for _not_ trying

- for trying?

My son is awesome, but our society is so messed up. We reward people for selfish defiance. When teenage pop stars prove they are "adults" by engaging in disgracefully explicit activities, they're rewarded with more money, attention, and affirmation. All this reinforcement of self-reliance can give people a sense of delusion that they're able to do whatever they want without consequences.

That's why adults are often stunned when things don't work out. When they encounter unexpected pressures of life, many grown*ups* are surprised that their self-security wasn't as strong as they had once thought; that they weren't as capable of facing difficulties on their own as they had believed; that they might actually need someone else's advice or help.

—always okay to ask for help

It takes a lot for an adult to admit inadequacy, by the way—which is why so many adults experience a midlife crisis.

3. CO-DEPENDENCE LEADS TO CHILDISHNESS

"Mine! Mine!" becomes the cry of an adulterated society.[18] How many times have you seen grown*ups* demand attention or special treatment? I've seen adults in restaurants act like spoiled brats if they weren't seated immediately or if the soup was too cold. People who are "co-dependent" tend to expect situations that make them feel happy instantly—and tend to discard anything that no longer adds speedy satisfaction.[19]

Because co-dependent adults feel free to do whatever they want (independence), they think anything that restricts their freedom should be resisted. And because they feel reliant upon themselves (self-dependence), they think anything that reveals their limitations should also be resisted. So don't be shocked if you hear the following comments coming from the mouth of a co-dependent adult:

- "I know it's wrong, but it makes me feel good."

- "I don't have to do what my boss says—he's an idiot."

- "When I get tired of this church, I can just shop for another one."

- "My vows don't really apply to me since my spouse has gotten out of shape."

- "Maybe just one more."

Feel free to write down some other childish adult statements you've heard:

- It's alright, Next time!

-

-

-

-

any others?

The problem with grown*ups* is that they have fallen prey to adulterated patterns of faith. They have been unfaithful to the way they were created to live.[20]

TILLING THE SOIL:

- What are you going to be like when you're older?

- What does it mean to grow older but not grow up?
  (Spread the word: #growdown)

- If you put a bunch of independent people in the room, what might happen?

- When does someone cross the line into false security?

- In the space below, draw a scene of what might happen when there are two co-dependent people but only one video game controller: What might that look like?

(draw a Picture mentally)

- Take a moment to pray about getting rid of bad habits. Be specific in your prayer. (God already knows about those habits, but it helps you recognize the areas where you need his help.)

CHAPTER 3:
YOU'RE GROWING THE WRONG WAY!

GROW
DOWN

There's a crazy scene in the 1987 movie *Planes, Trains, and Automobiles*. Late in the night, two very tired guys, Del and Neal, are driving on the highway, trying to get home for the holidays.[21] They seem to be humming along in the right direction until a driver from another car starts honking at them. Annoyed, Del simply honks back. But the other driver rolls down his window and starts yelling at Del and Neal, "You're going the wrong way!!!"

Neal, in the passenger seat, rolls down his window and yells back, "What?" The other driver frantically yells again, "You're going the wrong way!!!" Neal casually repeats what he'd heard to Del, "He says we're going the wrong way." Del responds, "How does he know where we're going?"

But the other driver won't relent: "You're going the wrong direction! You're going to kill somebody! You're going the wrong way!!!" Just then Neal notices that the driver is yelling at them from across the median strip in the opposite lanes of traffic! As awareness spreads over his face, semi-truck horns start blaring and four headlights start coming right at them. In that panicked moment, as they crash between two 18-wheelers, Neal looks over at Del, who suddenly is laughing and is dressed in the famous red costume of the devil, with his pointy tail and pitchfork.[22]

Our society has been driving in the wrong direction for a long time. It has been obsessed with the idea that real life begins at adulthood. Sadly, the drone of "When are you going to grow *up*?" has steered people away from the discovery of true life.

Think about it this way: When adults were younger, they were full of passion, imagination, hope, and wonder. But as they grew *up*, their enthusiasm was replaced by apathy. Perhaps they forgot the incredible potential available to them. Perhaps they began to worry about what others might think of them if they lived for God instead of living by the routines everyone else seemed to be following.

What child ever worries about that?

If people try to tell you that growing *up* is the goal for a Christian, inform them that a church of grown*ups* is a boring and unfruitful church. We don't need any more people who call themselves "disciples" of Jesus but who think their time of enjoying and stretching and growing has been accomplished.

But be careful here: This book is not a rebellion against older people. I believe strongly that older people can be (and should be) among the coolest and most God-honoring people on the planet (and I hope you intend on being one of those someday yourself). And even if we have to wear diapers again when we get older, I also believe that as we age we have a responsibility to get rid of childish behaviors in our lives.[23]

But unfortunately, our society associates growing older with growing *up*—and growing *up* with child*ish*ness. That's the error. How can people be faithful to Jesus when they add stuff to their lives like life-sucking debt and broken behaviors? It's tough enough to navigate a complex world of sexual options, pornography, divorces, abuse, lies, violence, cheating, scandals, betrayals, disappointments, temptations, and all the countless other things that batter against personal character, thrash against marriages, erode genuine love, and fight against the ability to stand strong in a stormy world. No wonder adults lose their childlike faith and substitute it with a childish one!

By growing *up,* adults have settled for a diminished experience of life.

In dramatic contrast to Twinkie-and-horse-lip faith, people who choose to **grow down** have tremendous hope and deep belief in God's involvement in this world. My 8-year-old daughter, for the last two years, has prayed this prayer at bedtime:

> *"Dear God, help there to be no earthquakes, floods, or tornadoes. Please help everyone to be healthy, help everyone in the whole world to be healthy. And help me have good dreams. Amen."*

Why don't adults pray like that? A.W. Tozer said it like this:

> *"Now, as always, God discovers Himself to 'babes' and hides Himself in thick darkness from the wise and prudent. We must simplify our approach to Him. We must strip down to essentials (and they will be found to be blessedly few). We must put away all effort to impress, and come with the guileless candor of childhood. If we do this, without a doubt God will quickly respond."*[24]

If you have grown *up* and have gotten sucked into the vortex of adulterated faith, be encouraged by people in the Bible who took simple corrective steps to turn around and begin growing in the right direction:

- In Psalm 51, an adulterated person begs God: "Re-create my heart!"

- In John 3, a fully grown man is instructed: "Be reborn!"

- In Romans 12:2, culturally conformed grown*ups* are told, "Instead of conforming to the patterns of your culture, be transformed by renewing your mind!"

It's time to rethink our society's preferred direction of growth. Stand against the pressure to add thing after thing, relationship after relationship, in search of fulfillment. Stay simple. Stay pure. You don't need more toys, more looks, more stresses, more romances, or more tantrums to discover the vitality of life that Jesus created you to have.

TILLING THE SOIL:

- How can growing *up* actually lead you further away from God?

- Look up the following verses and put a check by the one who follows God more naturally:

SCRIPTURE	CHILD	ADULT
Psalm 131:1-2	✓	
Proverbs 1:8-19	✓	
Matthew 11:25		✓
John 1:12-13	✓	
Galatians 4:6-7	✓	
Ephesians 5:1-2	✓	
Philippians 2:15		
Hebrews 12:7	✓	
1 Peter 1:14		
1 John 5:1-5		

- Are there any adult patterns in your own life right now that need to be redirected?

- Take a moment to write a childlike prayer to God. Pray about whatever comes to your mind, no matter how simple and pure. *(Spread the word: #growdown)*

PART II:
GROW DOWN

*Let your roots **grow down** into Christ...*

CHAPTER 4:
GREATEST IN THE KINGDOM

GROW
DOWN

The disciples were arguing—again.

"He called me 'the Rock'!" one of them said.

"Yeah, and he also called you the devil!" said another.

"Jesus loves me more than he loves all of you!" argued
another disciple. Side note: why world is cruel, broken –
think because certain moments
in life God loves them less

"Hey, he trusts me with the money!" said another.

"Yeah, but you're a cheat!" declared one of the other
disciples, taxingly.

This argument circled around and around for a while until
these young adults all agreed to ask the Master, who, mind
you, also happened to be the Ruler of the kingdom of
heaven. "Jesus," they propositioned, "which one of *us* is the
greatest in the kingdom of heaven?"

Of all the stupid, arrogant, envious, childish questions to
ask! Did they really just ask Jesus, the great I Am, which
one of *them* was the greatest in the kingdom of heaven?
Were they so self-absorbed that they forgot about Jesus, the
Creator, the King of kings and Lord of lords? Their argument
was so absolutely blasphemous that if I had been Jesus, in
that moment I would have opened up a good, ole-fashioned
can of smite upon their heads!

GREATEST IN THE KINGDOM

But Jesus had (and still has) a bit more composure than I have. Matthew 18 tells the story of his answer to their adulterated question this way:

> Jesus called a **little child** to him and put the child among them. Then he said, "I tell you the truth, unless you turn from your sins and **become like little children,** you will never get into the Kingdom of Heaven. So anyone who **becomes as humble as this little child** is the greatest in the Kingdom of Heaven. And anyone who welcomes a little child like this on my behalf is welcoming me. But if you cause one of these little ones who trusts in me to fall into sin, it would be better for you to have a large millstone tied around your neck and be drowned in the depths of the sea."[25]

It has always been the pursuit of adulthood to rise to the top, to get ahead, to climb the ladder. This was the assumption of the disciples. Jesus picked them, they assumed, because there must be something spectacular about them. Maybe they felt strongly independent or securely self-dependent. Maybe in their co-dependence they were seeking personal affirmation. Whatever the case, each one of them was selfishly arguing for status, grandeur, and other explicit grownup goals.[26]

Jesus wasn't impressed:

1. First point: Because the disciples were arrogant, Jesus suggests they might not even make it into the kingdom of heaven!

2. Second point: According to Jesus, the greatest in the kingdom of heaven is someone who becomes as humble as a little child. In other words, it is people of childlike faith, not adulterated faith, whom Jesus lifts up.[27]

3. Third point: Jesus identifies himself with a kid.[28] Ironic, then, that people keep striving to become adults. *wanna grow up?*
yes but should be no

4. Fourth point: Jesus takes innocence of faith in a person's heart very seriously. So if someone messes with a kid's faith, Jesus says it's just like messing with him. Jesus doesn't want anyone steering a child away from a pure love with God.

The person who causes a kid to grow *up* by adulterating that kid is going to get leveled with a nasty consequence by God. Jesus paints a terrible picture here for the adult who ruins a young person's life of faith: "It would be better," Jesus said, "for that person to be thrown into the sea with a large millstone tied around the neck."

Better than what? It's as if Jesus left his audience hanging with an unfinished thought. A millstone was a huge circular stone that was used to crush grain. It was also occasionally used as a means of execution! By attaching someone's neck to the stone and then throwing it into deep water, death occurred by broken neck and drowning. And this would be better than the consequence Jesus says is coming to the person who corrupts a child's walk with God. I believe that in his mercy Jesus didn't finish the sentence; it would have been too devastating for the adulterated disciples to hear.

This is like a scene out of *The Godfather*. So incensed that someone would dare harm one of his children, God the Father, in a Don Corleone raspy voice, declares, "If any of you tangles with one of my kids, you'll wish you were wearing concrete shoes in the Hudson River..."

A truly mature faith is not adulterated; it is childlike: innocent, joyous, simple, passionate, sweet-hearted, full of life. A child's arms can lift up the heaviest soul. A child's smile can melt the coldest heart. A child's heart and faith can move mountains.

- Met people like that
- always Smiling looking positive

BABIES ON A PLANE!

A baby once attacked my flight from Chicago to Minneapolis.

The scene: The plane was packed with grumpy, tired, anxious, sweaty, and sick grown*ups*. After having been delayed for a couple of hours at O'Hare International Airport, virtually every passenger was irritable.

That's when the baby's power began a course of action that would transform people's lives for the duration of the flight.

This cute little infant in the front rows gave one of the flight attendants a smile. It probably wasn't even intentional; more like a cute baby-belch or diaper-toot. But the flight attendant, drawn by the awesomeness of this little guy, got permission from the parents to hold the baby.

That gassy little creature started to giggle its belly and bobble its head and twinkle its eyes. And as the attendant walked him up and down the rows in her arms, the baby spread a freedom of life among the packed-in, sardined adults. That little baby, get this, actually had the audacity to start making eye contact with the passengers. And it wasn't long before every uptight, selfish, complaining passenger had been transformed into a gooey ball of joyful mush. As this baby babble-talked its way from row to row, any sense of frustration or self-concern melted away. Ego-absorbed travelers made silly goo-goo noises. Tuned-out, headphone-wearing tightwads made silly, funny faces. The formerly frustrated passengers were mesmerized by the exuberant power of this baby. Adults surrendered to the gentle might of a child.

> **Psalm 8:2 says this:** *You have taught children and infants to tell of your strength, silencing your enemies and all who oppose you.*

A mature faith is *un*adulterated, it is childlike, and it is powerful.

-leader
-wakes up
everyday wanting
to make difference

GROWING DOWN:

- If Jesus would have finished his thought in Matthew 18, what do you think he would have said?

  -temptation - follow other Christ followers

  - forgiveness- learn to look past flaws, learn from past mistakes

- Draw a comic strip about a baby's power.
  (Spread the word: #growdown)

```




```

```




```

```




```

```




```

- In the chart below, explore the differences between child*ish* faith and child*like* faith by adding your ideas to each column:

CHILDISH FAITH	CHILDLIKE FAITH
Spoiled	Thankful
	Pure thoughts
Sour attitude	
Pessimism	Optimism / Hope
	Wide-eyed wonder
	Trusting
	Imaginative
Junkie	
Bored, then bouncing, then bored, then bouncing, then bored, then…	
Plays selfishly	

- Take a moment to pray that God will help you recapture a childlike faith.

CHAPTER 5:
ROOTED IN CHRIST

GROW
DOWN

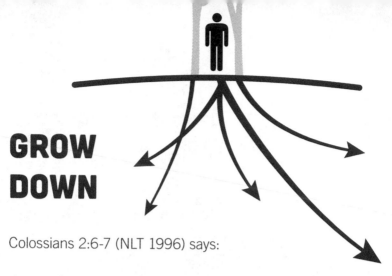

GROW DOWN

Colossians 2:6-7 (NLT 1996) says:

*Just as you accepted Christ Jesus as your Lord, continue to live in obedience to him. Let your roots **grow down** into him...*

ACCEPTING JESUS

When a seed is planted in fertile soil, the seed accepts the soil and the soil accepts the seed. If a seed ever refused to accept the soil, we would conclude that it was a ludicrous seed because it could never then become what it was created to become.

The word for "accepted" is one of the greatest words of the Bible. It's the idea that when you are offered a gift, you wrap your arms around that gift and draw it into yourself.

I remember getting a Star Wars Death Star set when I was about 10 years old. It had the trash compacter with the one-eyed monster, the rope swing, the planet-destroying gun, the elevator, and the light saber scene with Obi-Wan Kenobi and Darth Vader. What a nerd. I know. And I don't care. I accepted that gift as my own.

That's the message in the book of Colossians: When you plant yourself in Jesus, you accept Jesus and he accepts you. Paul sums it all up in chapter 3, verse 11: *Christ is all that matters, and he lives in all of us.*

Paul wrote this letter to people in a town called Colosse who had embraced Jesus. A guy named Epaphras had chosen to follow Jesus and then went back home to Colosse to tell everyone he knew.[29] As a result of his testimony, many people believed and embraced Jesus in their lives. Paul was saying, "Epaphras told me all about how you have accepted Jesus. Way to go!"

Choosing to follow Jesus is the most important step we could ever take. Jesus opened up his arms to take all of our crud — our sin, our shame, our weakness, our insecurity, and our worry — on the cross so that we could accept him as our Lord.[30]

Three simple, childlike phrases are all we need to be planted into Jesus. They are very difficult for adulterated people to say because they're among the most mature words humans could ever speak:

Sorry.

Thank you.

Please.

If you'd like to begin following Jesus, you can use the following prayer with those three powerful phrases:

> "Jesus, I accept you as the Lord of my life today. I am **SORRY** for my sins. **THANK YOU** for dying on the cross and forgiving me of my sins. **PLEASE** come into my life so that I can live for you."

If you've prayed that prayer, you have become part of a radical community of people. "Radical" means "root." So if you've decided to follow Jesus, you have begun to live a truly radical life.

- **If you have chosen to follow Jesus, find someone else who has made that same decision and share**

your good news. Ask them to pray for you and
help you to keep growing down into Jesus.
(Spread the word: #growdown)

ROOTING INTO JESUS

There's a rumor that one of my great-great-great-great
uncles was a radical named Johnny Appleseed. Have you
ever heard the legend? Maybe you've sung his song:

> Oooooh, the Lord's been good to me / and so I thank
> the Lord / for giving me the things I need / the sun
> and the rain and the apple seed / The Lord's been
> good to me / Amen, Amen, Amen, Amen, Amen.

Johnny Appleseed was born as John Chapman in 1774.[31]
He traveled across the pioneer lands of Pennsylvania, Ohio,
Indiana, and Illinois to help people learn about Jesus and
to help them have food to eat. So on his travels he planted
orchards of apples and pears, and ministered to thousands
of people in need. At first, many people laughed at his slow
work: traveling by foot and planting seeds that would take
years to produce fruit. But his patient endurance paid off.
By the time he died in 1845, his impact was famous.

Have you ever watched a seed become a tree? It takes endurance! This is hard for our fast-paced, grown*up* world to accept. We want an "A" without study, fast food without preparation, sex without marriage, relationship without commitment—and then we wonder why our lives feel unproductive.

A Jesus-centered life takes determined patience. Eventually the radical life will explode with abundance, but it is a long process that changes our identity, our integrity, and our interaction.

Identity: Our identity has to do with who we are. "Christ is your real life," Paul wrote to the Colossians.[32] By rooting ourselves into Jesus, we receive a new identity based in Jesus. We no longer have to listen to the soul-eroding lies that we aren't special or worthy—because Jesus assures us that he loves us completely.[33]

Integrity: Our integrity has to do with what we do. Here's what Paul wrote: *Whatever you do or say, do it as a representative of Jesus.*[34] A life centered in Jesus exterminates its adulterated patterns, like the ones Paul lists in Colossians: sexual sins, greed, rage, maliciousness, slander, foul language, and lying.[35]

In place of these things, our integrity is nourished through a depth of relationship with Christ. *You will grow as you learn to know God better and better (Colossians 1:10).* In place of any bad habits of faith, **growing down** into Jesus creates new behaviors in us—such as prayer, compassion, patience, thankfulness, and discernment.[36] A.W. Tozer wrote:

> *"The man who has struggled to purify himself and has had nothing but repeated failures will experience real relief when he stops tinkering with his soul and looks to the perfect One. While he looks at Christ, the very things he has so long been trying to do will be getting done within him. It will be God working in him to will and to do."* [37]

Interaction: Our interaction has to do with our impact on others. Those who are rooted in Christ end up changing the world.[38] They learn to support families faithfully, to conduct businesses ethically, and to treat people justly.[39] As our identity and integrity are formed in Christ, we commit deeply to relationships and to the welfare of others in all circumstances, even the most difficult ones.[40]

LEARNING JESUS

God doesn't care how old you are. God wants every person, at every moment of life, to be learning. A "disciple" is literally a person who learns. A "learner" is someone who keeps growing in what they know and who they are. A disciple doesn't stop growing in Jesus.

You've heard this old adage: "You can't teach an old dog new tricks." Well, the moral of this story is that grown*ups* often get stuck in their ways. Adults tend to think of themselves as people who have ended their journey of education and dependence. Consider these examples of fully grown adults who had to be dramatically taught to keep learning:

- At a full age, Abraham and Sarah laughed at God when they were told he had a new plan for them.[41]

- At 80 years old, Moses was quite a "mature adult" when God gave him a risky new mission.[42]

- Jesus chewed out the Pharisees because, even though they thought they had everything figured out, they were actually immature in their faith.[43]

- Peter learned that when he grew older, he would have to follow God where he wouldn't want to go.[44]

- Having reached a pinnacle of learning, the highly successful Saul was knocked down by Jesus' brilliant calling to become a disciple.[45]

And then there are the examples of young people who God used so mightily:

- Joshua and Caleb, two younger-generation leaders, believed God could defeat the "giants" in the land while all the older leaders cowered in fear.[46]

- Samuel, a young boy, was the only one in Israel who could hear God's voice.[47]

- Mary, a humble teenage girl, was chosen to carry the Son of God.[48]

- The disciples, a ragtag collection of young adults, learned to follow Jesus and transform the world.

- Timothy and Titus, young leaders, were vibrantly effective in a rapidly growing church of the first century.

Then there was David. As a teenager, he defeated enemies who had immobilized even the most seasoned adult warriors. He did this because he constantly deepened his relationship with God. Faithful followers of Jesus learn that *"what is impossible for people is possible with God."*[49]

But when David grew *up,* he started following his own desires instead of God's desires. He stopped learning and then committed *adultery.* As a result, it took a violent jolt to his heart to snap him back into the process of growing with God again.[50]

How can we keep ourselves from growing *up* like David did? How can we be sure to keep rooting our lives more deeply into Jesus?

NINE WAYS TO GROW DOWN INTO JESUS

There are many ways to build a Jesus-centered life. Here are a few tips you can try:

> **1. Pray** – Just start talking with God all the time in your own words about everything in your life. Also take

some time at least once a week to pray with other Christians, too.

2. **Read your Bible** – Just start reading your Bible. Read through the book of Mark to discover some of the exciting things about Jesus, or the book of Acts to learn about the first Christians, or the book of Judges to read about nasty stuff, or Philippians to be encouraged. Also take some time at least once a week to study the Bible with other Christians, too.

3. **Talk about your faith** – Talk about your faith with people who know Jesus and people who don't. Ask God to give you courage and wisdom, but most of all, an overflowing heart for others.

4. **Go on a mission trip** – Experience what God is doing in other places of the world among people who are different from you.

5. **Worship** – Be sure to worship God every day. You can praise God any time, spontaneously or through times like morning devotionals. Also take some time each week to gather with other Christians to sing songs of worship together.

6. **Appreciate creation** – Get outside for a walk. Sit under the shade of a tree. Jump into a lake on a summer's day. Snowboard down a mountain. Breathe in the air and take in spectacular views. Taking time to notice creation can help you be in awe of God's work and remind you of the care God has for you.

7. **Serve others** – Jesus came to serve. So a Jesus-centered person serves others, too. Work at a food shelter, pick up leaves for an elderly person, make your bed, clean up the dishes, and be the first one to wipe up a spill. Do things without needing to be asked or noticed. And do it all in the name of Jesus.

8. **Teach younger people about Jesus** – Perhaps the best way to keep learning is to start teaching. Volunteer in a children's ministry, guide your younger siblings to a deeper faith, baby-sit, or help lead Vacation Bible School.

9. **Read more books like this one** – If you find that books like this help you grow in faith, either on your own or by going through it with a small group, then find some more resources like this.[51]

GROWING DOWN:

Grow Down With Psalm 1: The psalms are meant to help us build a life rooted in God. For this reason, the very first psalm begins with a visual image that we're supposed to keep in mind. Look at the first three verses of the book of Psalms:

> *Blessed is the one*
> > *who does not walk in step with the wicked*
> *or stand in the way that sinners take*
> > *or sit in the company of mockers,*
> *but whose delight is in the law of the Lord,*
> > *and who meditates on his law day and night.*
>
> *That person is like a* **tree** *planted by streams of*
> > *water, which yields its fruit in season*
> *and whose leaf does not wither—*
> > *whatever they do prospers.*[52]

- Compare Colossians 2:6-7 with Psalm 1:1-3. What similarities and differences do you see?

- How does Psalm 1:1-2 fit into the first five chapters of this book?

- How do you think verse 3 might fit with the rest of this book?

- Which of the "nine ways to **grow down** into Jesus" will you try to make a regular part of your life this week? *(Spread the word: #growdown)*

CHAPTER 6:
UNLIMITED GROWTH & UNLIMITED RESOURCES

GROW
DOWN

[handwritten: with God]
[handwritten: eper ... eeper your roots go]

If I were to stand on my own two feet, how far could I grow? I'm only 5'6" (though I know you must have been imagining that I was at least 6'1", right?). I have some shortcomings when it comes to growing *up* in my own abilities.[53] Using some talent and motivation, I could probably develop some decent coping skills. But eventually even those will give way to some other stronger pressures (such as stress, illness, hurt, and so on).

[handwritten: -Tree roots grow around]
[handwritten: road blocks so should we]

Each of us has a limited capacity in our own power. As we grow *up* we discover that we just can't grow enough independently to overcome our own inadequacies.[54] We may learn to stand on our own two feet, but then the world beats us back down.

[handwritten: -move out - still need advice, help from parents, friendships?]

True life, however, roots deeply into the unlimited resources of Christ. He's an eternal energy reservoir. Think about this: If you were to stand in Jesus, how far could you grow? How much capacity does Jesus have?

[handwritten: comments?]

Ephesians 3:17-19 says it like this: *Your roots will **grow down into God's love and keep you strong**. And may you have the power to understand, as all God's people should, **how wide, how long, how high, and how deep** his love is. May you experience the love of Christ, **though it is too great to understand fully.***

Imagine if you were just a wee human standing on a big circle that represented Jesus. Then imagine that this circle was filled with all the infinite resources of God, rich with nutrients. Your growth potential would be limitless because you could root into everything you would ever need to grow for eternity.

JESUS

It is an extreme understatement to say that Jesus is amazing. Too wonderful for words, there could never be enough written about his glory. In Colossians, Paul takes a moment to try to describe just a little bit of the extent of the wondrous reality of Christ:[55]

- He is the visible image of the invisible God

  means heis our model on how to live life even know heis not physically here

- Existed before everything else came into being

- Supreme ruler in charge of creation

- Creator of everything there is (seen and unseen)

- Everything exists for him

- Holds everything together (otherwise it would spin out of control)

- Gives life after death

- The fullness of God dwells in him

- He reconciles everything to himself through his death on the cross[56]

A thousand years ago, a monk named Anselm of Canterbury tried to describe how amazing Jesus is, so he wrote this mind-bending prayer: "Now we believe that You are something than which nothing greater can be thought."[57] Confused? Well, that's because Jesus is beyond our ability to comprehend. Because we are rooted in Jesus, our growth potential is unlimited and our years on Earth are a chance to discover how great eternity with Jesus is going to be.

I used to think that once we got to heaven, we would be fully developed, done growing, totally complete. In some ways this is true, I suppose. The Bible does talk about how the follower of God will be sanctified and made new.[58] Psalm 119:96 indicates that even perfection has its limits, yet God's commands are boundless. I now think that God is so amazing that we're going to wake up every day in heaven and discover something new and deep and marvelous about our Creator.[59] We will never stop growing in our knowledge and relationship with God. Each day in heaven I think we'll wake up and say, "Lord, we didn't know that about you! You are amazing!" We will never know him so well that we could say, "Meh, we've got you figured out."

Are you short on patience? Jesus has an unlimited reserve of that. Are you short on joy? Jesus has more than you could handle. Are you short on confidence? Yep, he's got that for you. Do you need help figuring out what to do in a hard situation? Jesus has unlimited wisdom, understanding, truth, and power to help you get through whatever you're facing.

"All Out of Love" is an old rock ballad by a group called Air Supply. (Never heard of the band? Ask your parents… or your grandparents.) Jesus would never have to sing that song! We will never hear Jesus say, "Sorry, I've got no mercy for you today. I'm all out. Spent it all on a bunch of jerks yesterday."

a feel of great pleasure and happiness

GROW DOWN:

- What amazes you about Jesus? **Stretch your artistic side:** Go back to page 61 and, underneath the man on the circle (which can't fit on the page because it's so huge!), draw roots extending down into Jesus—and then jot down all the resources you can think of that Jesus has for us. If you're having any trouble thinking up some of these, you can skim through the book of John or read through the psalms that David wrote. There are also some examples in the back of this book.[60] *(Spread the word: #growdown)*

- Take a moment to praise Jesus for his infinite greatness.

come back
prayer

- Think of 12 different things about Jesus that you'd like
  to **grow down** into this year, one for each month:

Step out of my comfort zone   January

Find a bible plan and follow   February
                         it

Find 31 bible versus   March
and stick one in my mind each day

Vollunteer 10 hours   April

spend 5 minutes in bible before social   May
                                    media
                                in morning

journal   June

memorize a a verse of Psalm   July   every
                                      day

focus on becoming a quick   August
                       for giver

take time to pray   September
     for 2 extra people each day (5)
start up a bible study   October

Sit in silence - reflect   November

read first 5 every   December
morning before
social media

PART III: DRAW UP

*...and **draw up** nourishment from Christ,*
being built strong and vigorous in the truth that
you've been taught...

GROW DOWN

CHAPTER 7:
STANDING STRONG
IN THE TRUTH

GROW
DOWN

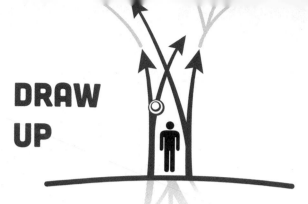

DRAW
UP

Last year I asked some college students who the "hottest" actor was. Immediately, one female student gushed, "Channing Tatum." I had to admit that I hadn't even heard of Channing Tatum. "Is that a human?" I asked, wondering why a person would be named "Channing."

So I searched online for this guy with the weird name, and then I quickly accepted the truth. I am not Channing Tatum—and he might not even be human. I don't have his features or his chiseled looks. (Nor, let me be very clear, do I have a man-crush on Channing Tatum.)

As I get older and look more like Methuselah than like Channing Tatum, I could be tempted to feel disappointed. "Not adequately equipped" is the old meaning to the word *disappointed*, and it's what the world concludes about us. We are all too nervous, too proud, or too worried. We are all imperfect, all sinners, all physically, emotionally, or socially awkward. All of us are creatures with cracks in our armor, and that includes Mr. Tatum.

BUILT STRONG IN CHRIST

But in Jesus is life that never perishes.[61] In him we are built strong and vigorous in the truth. In Christ we are able to **draw up** everything we need to truly live.[62] Those who dig themselves down deep into the Lord will stand in his strength. *I am like an olive tree, thriving in the house of God (Psalm 52:8).*

In Matthew 7, Jesus says that anyone who listens to and obeys him is *"like a person who builds a house on solid rock."* When the winds beat against the house, he promises that *"it won't collapse."*[63] The point is that people who secure themselves down into Christ will **draw up** strength to stand through torrential storms of life. Proverbs 10:25 says it like this: *When the storms of life come, the wicked are whirled away, but the godly have a lasting foundation.*

There is nothing else worth basing ourselves on than Jesus Christ. No other person, no other place, no other thing, and no other idea should ever serve as an alternative to Jesus as the foundation for our lives.

VIGOROUS IN THE TRUTH

The Old English word for tree is *treow*, which is where we get the word *true*. Something that is true is "a deeply planted idea."[64] Truth is vigorous. It is living and active. It is freeing and empowering. And when we **grow down** into Jesus, truth is what we are taught.

We learn the truth, first of all, from God. The Lord speaks, he tells us in Isaiah 48. The psalms tell us that the Lord is near to all who call on him in truth.[65] Jesus declared that he himself is *"the truth"* in John 14:6. The Holy Spirit is called the *"Spirit of Truth"* who guides us *"into all truth"* in John 16:13.

We also learn the truth from other followers of Jesus. Psalm 15:2 says that people who are blameless speak truth from their hearts. In Proverbs 12:17, honest witnesses tell truth that endures. Truthful witnesses save lives, according to Proverbs 14:25. A loving relationship rejoices in truth, says the famous "love" chapter, 1 Corinthians 13. So no matter what you are experiencing in your life, whether it is a season of calm, of excitement, or of storm, you can share in the joy and security and source of life that is found in no one or nothing other than Christ.

Drawing up Christ's resources will build us to start looking like Jesus in the way we live and act. Paul told Timothy: *Don't let anyone think less of you because you are young. Be an example to all believers in what you say, in the way you live, in your love, your faith, and your purity.*[66] When people see us, they'll begin to see Jesus in us because we are **drawing up** his characteristics into our own lives.

The truth builds us in strength so we can stand against anything the world could throw at us. As author and pastor Francis Chan recently wrote: "We serve a King who has absolute authority over every square inch of creation.... Understanding this truth should give us confidence as we move out into a world that is opposed to God's reign."[67]

So keep Jesus in your heart and your heart in Jesus. This pattern of truth will enable you to stand tall through anything. In Philippians 4:12-13, Paul said this: *I know how to live on almost nothing or with everything. I have learned the secret of living in every situation, whether it is with a full stomach or empty, with plenty or little. For I can do everything through Christ, who gives me strength.*

DRAW UP:

- If you could have a conversation with Channing Tatum about truth, what would you ask and say? Why? *(Spread the word: #growdown)*

- When something is deeply rooted in fertile soil, what happens above the surface?

- What can you learn about truth from the Old English word for tree?

- Who in your life serves as a good role model of the truth? Who are you a good role model of truth for?

- In what ways does society look down on young people? How could being strong and vigorous in the truth help change this attitude?

- In the space below, write yourself a letter from God's perspective. What truth does God want to strengthen you with today?

- Take a moment to pray. Ask God to help you **draw up** what you need from him today.

CHAPTER 8:
WITHSTANDING WINDS

GROW DOWN

WITHSTANDING WINDS

My dog's name is Smudge. He's a cute beagle/spaniel mix and a rescue dog. He's loyal, stays in our yard, fetches things for fun, and wags his tail at me as if I'm the greatest friend he could have. I like him. He's nice. He's certainly much better than a cat could ever be. (Sorry, cat fans.) There was one day when I wasn't very proud of him, though. I had planted this little 1-foot-tall blue spruce tree with tiny roots. Declaring it "good," I turned to get cleaned up. That's when Smudge trotted over to me, tail wagging, drooling dirt and needles from his mouth. "Smudge, have you eaten from the tree of blue and spruce?" I cried.

Many people would like to live a rooted life but find the pressures of keeping Jesus at the center of their lives to be agonizing. It seems to them that it would be easier to just get knocked over. On all sides of Colossians 2:6-7 are verses indicating that people who live faithfully will be under attack. Jesus warns his disciples about persecutions, temptations, and frustrations. To stand firm in the truth is not an easy task. Read

The emerald ash borer (EAB) is an invasive beetle that swarms and destroys ash trees. EAB larvae feed on the inside of the bark, in effect sabotaging the transportation of water and nutrients from the root of the tree to the trunk and branches. Since it was discovered in 2002, the EAB has spread through one-third of North America and has killed tens of millions of ash trees.[68]

Like Smudge or the EAB, the winds of culture batter against truth. So Paul reminds the Colossians that no matter what, Jesus has enabled them to stand.[69] Paul doesn't want them to be deceived by *empty philosophies and high-sounding nonsense.*[70] Instead, he tells them to remember that they are made complete in Christ. Because of that, they don't need to falter.[71]

Sometimes, like hurricanes or tornadoes, these winds cause damage and thrash apart lives and tear through faith. Other times, maybe more often than not, the winds are like the steady, eroding winds that slowly over the years wear against a person's stamina and endurance. In the end, whether by hurricane or erosion, the blowing diversions of our world can eventually knock us off the foundation of our faith if we aren't well-rooted in Christ.

If any of you are like me (please don't take that as an insult!), then you're hit daily with the pressure winds of this life: big decisions, hectic activities, responsibilities, illness, busyness, worries, soul searching—aaaagggghhhh!!! Sometimes I get so gut-wrenchingly exhausted that I feel like I'm going to fall apart. You know, even the winds of the pressures of time have been taking a toll on me personally lately—as I keep losing hair on top of my head and I keep finding it reappearing in my ears! I'm feeling some strong wind burn physically!

So rather than being surprised, we can prepare for the winds and be able to stand even taller by rooting even more deeply into Jesus. Try this: *In the left column on the next page, brainstorm all the "winds" you think could blow against you this year (such as bullying, sexual pressures, identity issues, depression, different temptations, and so on). Then, in the right column, brainstorm the resources Jesus has that you could draw up to help you withstand those winds:*

WINDS	JESUS' RESOURCES

-peer pressure
   - clothing
   - hair
   - new trends
   * spirit week
- not enough sleep
   - push prayers off
- media
- skyward
   - grades
- images of perfect body
- requirements in gym
   - baseline tests
* possible breakups
   - close friend
   - boyfriend/
       girlfriend
	- youthgroup
	- Christian friends
	- role models
	- prayers
	- deep silence moments
	- deep breaths
	- bible study
	- church
	   - sunday mornings
	- hanging out
	   with friends
	   - back to great
	     role models
	- reading a good book
	- excercise

Look back at your list and circle the hurricane-force winds. These are the intense pressures that crush against people (such as divorce, eating disorders, suicidal thoughts, and so on). Now go back to your list and highlight the slow-eroding winds. These are the things that slowly impact someone over time, perhaps without them even realizing (such as self-esteem, grudges, media, loneliness, and so on). This list of winds could feel pretty overwhelming.

But the good news is that Jesus' resources are stronger! When we go through something difficult, that's precisely when we can **grow down** into Jesus so we can **draw**

up what we need. We might feel like fragile jars of clay, but when we are in Jesus, then what is in us is an all-surpassing power. As 2 Corinthians 4:8-9 proclaims: *We are pressed on every side by troubles, but we are not crushed. We are perplexed, but not driven to despair. We are hunted down, but never abandoned by God. We get knocked down, but we are not destroyed.*

Listen to this now: The good news is that you can stand through anything that comes against you if you **draw up** nourishment from Jesus because he is the source of all life, of all strength, and of all truth. With your footing in him, you will not be moved by the winds that blow against you because they cannot rattle Christ. Psalm 33:11 proclaims this: *The Lord's plans stand firm forever; his intentions can never be shaken.* - God's plan for us will not change because of what we believe

No wind can shake the foundations of heaven, let alone rattle God. No economic crisis can unnerve God or cause him worry about his future. No storm can cause God fear. No illness can wreck God. No enemy can surprise God. No situation can stress God beyond what he can bear. So cast your burdens upon him. Trust deeply in him.

The floods have risen up, O Lord. The floods have roared like thunder; the floods have lifted their pounding waves.

But mightier than the violent raging of the seas, mightier than the breakers on the shore—the Lord above is mightier than these! (Psalm 93:3-4).

If you are being blown about today, let your roots **grow down** into Christ. The unshakable God is ready for you to **draw up** the nourishment and strength you need. Don't try to stand on your own —you'll end up as a tumbleweed.

DRAW UP:

- Where does a tumbleweed come from?

- Earlier in the chapter, you identified specific winds and Jesus' resources that can help you during those times. How can you seek and obtain those resources from him?

- What truth have you learned about God that you really need to root into this week? *(Spread the word: #growdown)*

- Take a moment to pray that God will give you strength against the winds you or your friends are facing today.

CHAPTER 9:
SCARS THAT BECOME BEAUTY MARKS

GROW DOWN

KNOT

Outside of a Starbucks a few years ago, someone shared with me the most difficult life situation I have ever heard.[72] As I listened to him explain why he felt like he was at the end of his life, I couldn't imagine what he was going through or how things would be OK. As gratified college students and good-looking career-types swapped lighthearted stories and purchased their skim-latte-no-whip-mocha-fraps, we both sat on a bench at a loss for words.

I silently prayed, "Lord, I don't know what to say. I've got nothing in me that could help him—and I'm worried he's got no hope."

Next to our bench was a gnarly tree growing out of the sidewalk: distressed, with knots and wounds, surrounded by a rusty iron grate, its trunk rubbed raw from bike chains, and prehistoric names carved into the bark. I felt God tugging me through this wretched tree.

"What do you notice about that tree?" I asked him.

"That tree's in bad shape," he said, "but it's beautiful."

"Beautiful?" I was shocked. In my grownup opinion, that tree should have been uprooted and mulched. "How is that tree beautiful?"

"Well, I know it doesn't look like much, but even in this harsh environment, it's fighting. Somehow it's still standing—and it's even alive and growing."

I was stunned. This hurting friend of mine was about to teach me an incredibly beautiful truth that would change my life. I urged him, "Keep going. What else do you see?"

"Every leaf has a unique print—none like the other," he continued. "The detail is inspiring. The roots must be strong, because they're starting to crack and push the concrete sidewalk. There's a new offshoot of a branch with a new bud on it. And look at that scar—how it healed to become a special marker for that tree. Gives it a lot of character.

"Ken," he stopped, "I'm the tree."

Never have I had a more inspirational coffee conversation at Starbucks. My friend gave his life to Jesus deeply that day, and I did, too! Everything wasn't fixed: The winds would still beat hard against his life. Yet he began to **draw up** incredible strength, and his wounds began to become beauty marks. Now as hurting people get to know him and the story he has lived, they can see that he's a source of incredible encouragement.

Our adult world would like to make us think we should not be blemished. If we have flaws, the grown*up* philosophy preaches, we should cover them up and hide them from others, or else run the risk that people will think something is wrong with us.

Yet faith in the way of Jesus embraces the concept of woundedness. Jesus took sin and pain and hurt upon himself, and now proudly bears the wounds for us to see.

Trees are beautiful. Yet every tree has knots.

As a kid, my favorite tree was the most scarred-up, gnarled-up tree in our yard. It was the best one to climb. There were places for my feet to set and places for my hands to hold. Here was a tree that had been scarred at different points in its life and, as a result, had grown large knots. So when I came along one day, looking for life, this tree was a blessing to me. I spent countless days in the arms of that tree, where I discovered imagination and hope and refuge and rest and play.

In the witness of mended wounds, people who are hurting find inspiration. The testimony of a scar that has become a beauty mark is one of restoration and healing—that is, a story of good news! It is evidence of God's restorative work in the lives of people who have been bent under the weight of the winds of this world.

The Bible is rich with people whose scars were turned into beauty marks by God. Here are just a few:

- **Joseph:** The tragedy of Joseph's childhood became the backdrop for one of the most vivid stories of life transformation the world has ever seen.

- **Moses:** God used Moses' speech impediment to dramatically speak to Pharaoh and to communicate God's greatest commands.

- **The Woman at the Well:** In John 4, Jesus offered restoration to a disgraced woman, who then shared this news with her whole village.

- **Paul:** In circumstances of weakness, Paul spoke about how Jesus sustained him and gave him strength.

- **Zacchaeus:** A sinner can't sin much more than this seedy tax collector. So in Luke 19, when he abundantly gave away his wealth to those he had wronged, his story became a symbol of salvation through Jesus.

- **Lazarus:** Talk about visible scars! In John 11, Lazarus walked out of his tomb and became a walking billboard of Jesus' ability to turn hurt into life.

OUR BEAUTIFULLY SCARRED SAVIOR

It's remarkable that even after his resurrection, Jesus presented himself with scars.[73] It's by his scars that we are healed. And as we **draw up** the resources of Christ, it's often by our healed scars that others find their way to Christ. The Bible says the journey is tough, but *"how beautiful are the feet of messengers who bring good news!"*[74]

I'm not saying this flippantly at all. It's only in the power of Jesus that this happens. Jesus takes our real pain and offers us healing so that we can flourish the way he wants us to flourish. He doesn't take the scar away, but he transforms it into a beauty mark.

Celebrating a scar in our culture doesn't make much sense. Billions of dollars are spent every year in our society to cover up any blemish. But the person who **grows down** into Jesus **draws up** a powerful truth—a truth that is wonderfully depicted in a song by Gungor called "Beautiful Things":[75]

> All this pain
> I wonder if I'll ever find my way?
> I wonder if my life could really change at all?
> All this earth
> Could all that is lost ever be found?
> Could a garden come up from this ground at all?

The song goes on to talk about how God makes beautiful things out of each of us, how he makes hope appear around, how he makes life from chaos—inspiring words that draw us back to Jesus.

DRAW UP:

- Have you ever known anyone whose life was transformed by Jesus? What was that person's story?

- Are there any scars in people's lives that Jesus can't transform into beauty marks? Why or why not?

- Take a moment to pray about the wounds you have and how Jesus could bring healing to you.

- In the space below, write or draw your testimony of God's work of healing in your life. Try not to emphasize the scars, but instead focus on the healing God gives. Try also to think of how your testimony could help someone else who has experienced a similar hurt. *(Spread the word: #growdown)*

PART IV:
GO OUT

*...and let your lives **overflow** in thanksgiving for all Christ has done.*

GROW DOWN

CHAPTER 10:
IF YOU CAN CONTAIN JESUS...

GROW DOWN

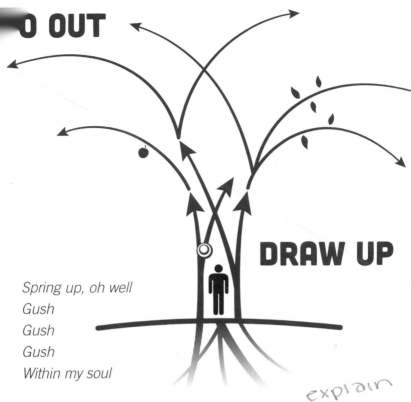

DRAW UP

Spring up, oh well
Gush
Gush
Gush
Within my soul

explain

Like a nuclear detonation, a volcanic explosion, or an oil pipeline bursting at the bottom of the sea, all the powers of the world cannot hold back the intense power of God. Those who **grow down** into Jesus and **draw up** strength from him will naturally **go out** into life with thanksgiving and fruitfulness.

In other words: If we can contain Jesus, then maybe we're not truly tapping into him.

IF YOU CAN CONTAIN JESUS...

In Acts 4, Peter and John got arrested. When the frustrated authorities told them to stop talking about Jesus, their response must have stunned the adulterated leaders present that day: "Uh, yeah, about that," Peter and John said. "You really don't seem to understand what's going on. We can't stop. We can't help it. It just overflows from us. We can't contain what's inside of us! We have to let Jesus out! If we don't, we'll rupture something!" Literally, they said, *"We cannot stop telling about everything we have seen and heard."* [76]

No wonder the early Christians changed the world!

EXPLOSIVE FAITH

This same Good News that came to you is going out all over the world. It is bearing fruit everywhere by changing lives, just as it changed your lives from the day you first heard and understood the truth about God's wonderful grace. [77]

Christianity, which began as a small gathering of 120 people one day in Jerusalem, exploded onto the world map. Within 30 years the seed of the gospel had rooted itself all over the Roman Empire. It was spreading so rapidly that the government felt the need to quell the movement. But even that couldn't stop it.

Paul probably wrote his letter to the Colossians while he was in prison for talking about Jesus. During his Jesus-centered life, he logged thousands of miles; endured dozens of beatings; spoke passionately to large crowds, politicians, and kings; and broke through formidable social and economic barriers along the way. Even under arrest, Paul continued to share his faith with prisoners and guards, with judges and rulers, all over the empire. And he wasn't alone. Numerous others were like him—people like Philip, Barnabas, Timothy and Titus, Epaphras, Lydia, Priscilla, Aquila, and many more. Back then people who heard about Jesus had to make a decision: Am I going to follow Jesus and lay my life on the line?

In that first generation, something made thousands upon thousands of people risk their lives in an abundant overflow of faith. "There was something so attractive and intriguing about this first group of believers," Francis Chan recently wrote. "Not only was the birth of this group miraculous, the way they began to live together and interact was something the world had never seen."[78] All over the world, the gospel was spreading and changing lives everywhere.

Imagine yourself in a city where hundreds of thousands of people had never heard the message about Jesus Christ. The city would have been filled with other gods,

look like?
could it be different then
we expect? good?

other morals, other systems, other ways of doing life. Then imagine that you decided to commit yourself to a growing movement based on a personal relationship with Jesus—not because your family had always gone to church on Christmas or Easter, but because you placed your trust in Jesus as Lord.

What could be said of the ancient world could be said of our postmodern world. The prevailing winds of our society involve countless other gods and options. And, sadly, far too many people who say they're Christians admit they don't have a vibrant relationship with Jesus.[79] Perhaps the saddest aspect of our culture's adulterated faith is the way that it squelches passion. It's as if people think faith is an on/off switch that is only momentarily flipped on when a toe gets stubbed in the dark. People have grown comfortable with a "faith" that attends church on Sunday morning but forgets about Jesus by lunchtime.

many people you can tell

With this in mind, Thom and Joani Schultz raise some provoking questions in their book *Why Nobody Wants to Go to Church Anymore:*[80]

- "Even though more than 90 percent of Americans say they believe in God, why did most of them avoid church last weekend?"[81]

- "Why are researchers predicting that by 2020 more than 85 percent of Americans won't worship God at church?"[82]

  — technology

- "Why has the percentage of young people attending church every week dropped to 15 percent?"[83]

  — reputations

- "If 88 percent of adults say their faith is important to them, why do the majority of them choose not to grow their faith in church?"[84]

  — a lot of consistent work towards it

Here's the deal: It is God's power that enables a mustard-seed-sized faith to move mountains.[85] In God, all things are made possible. We can't really do much in our own strength to change the landscape of faith in this world. That's why Jesus told his disciples, *"You will receive power when the Holy Spirit comes upon you. And you will be my witnesses, telling people about me everywhere…to the ends of the earth."*[86]

We desperately need a new generation who will **grow down** into Jesus, **draw up** his truth, and **go out** with his life.[87]

— how do we do that?

There is so much power in Jesus, and I think we don't allow ourselves to tap into the unlimited growth we could experience in him—or the unlimited potential we have in him—because we still keep trying to stand on the surface with our two feet. If we refuse to **grow down,** we may never know the explosive extent of power that is so near, so ready to be discovered.

Why is our generation so afraid to put down the phones for an hour and go to church? Why is our generation scared of Jesus?

GO OUT:

- Have you ever been encouraged by someone with a dynamic faith? What did they do that inspired you? *go forth and actually develop a relationship*

- Why do you think many Christians don't seem to be overflowing with life nowadays?

- In what specific ways would you like to overflow with life from God?

Extra bible verse!

- Checklist: Ways to overflow this week (add your own ideas to the list) *(Spread the word: #growdown)*

  ☐ Send someone an encouraging note.

  ☐ Say something nice to someone today.

  ☐ Thank your mom for something she's done recently.

☐ Pray for someone who is sick.

☐ Spend less and give more.
   — bibles at youth group

☐ Help a neighbor move furniture.

☐ Help a friend with their homework.

☐ Hold the door open for the person behind you.

☐ _____

☐ _____

☐ _____

☐ _____

☐ _____

☐ _____

☐ _____

☐ _____

- Take a moment to pray about what action step you could take to bless the world today.
   — pray for person to right

- Colossians 2:7

- Proverbs 4:23
    - Learn from
         mistakes
    - pop culture
        -> learn
         towards
          those types
          of actions

- Proverbs 22:6

CHAPTER 11:
THE OVERFLOWING LIFE

GROW
DOWN

Jesus cursed a fig tree. It was a good-looking, leafy fig tree. But as Jesus stepped in for a closer look, he discovered the fig tree had a problem. It had no figs. It was fruitless. So Jesus cursed the tree.[88]

Then Jesus cursed the Temple. I guess you could say he was having a bad day.

The Temple was busy with religious activity and looked healthy and vibrant. But as Jesus stepped in for a closer look, he discovered the Temple had a problem. Hearts were distracted, and faith bowed to consumerism. The Temple, no longer rooted in God, had become a fruitless place. Alarmingly, Jesus overturned the selling tables and drove out those associated with the unfaithful system. *"The Scriptures declare, 'My Temple will be called a house of prayer for all nations,' but you have turned it into a den of thieves" (Mark 11:17).*

The next morning Jesus and his disciples passed by the fig tree from the day before. The disciples were shocked to see that this fruitless fig tree had completely shriveled up and died! Mark notes that the tree had withered *from the roots* up.[89] It couldn't **draw up** the nutrition it needed to live.

No matter how impressive it looks, if a generation rejects the opportunity to **grow down** into the soil of God's marvelous love and **draw up** life from him, that generation will be barren. I fear that when Jesus looks closely at our expression of Christianity today, he discovers the lack of fruit stemming from our shallow root system. God is not pleased at all with those who claim to be religious but who are actually only dressed *up*.[90]

Jesus once declared this: *"A good tree produces good fruit, and a bad tree produces bad fruit. A good tree can't produce bad fruit, and a bad tree can't produce good fruit. So every tree that does not produce good fruit is chopped down and thrown into the fire" (Matthew 7:17-19).* In other words, faithlessness produces fruitlessness, and fruitlessness produces nothing good.

FRUIT

The good news is that people who are rooted in Jesus bring true benefit to the world. In Jesus we become natural producers of overflowing life. (Notice that I didn't say a comfortable life, or a no-problem life; I said an *overflowing life*.) Psalm 92:12-14 says this:

But the godly will flourish like palm trees
and grow strong like the cedars of Lebanon.
For they are transplanted to the Lord's own house.
They flourish in the courts of our God.
Even in old age they will still produce fruit;
they will remain vital and green.

The fruit of the Spirit is love, joy, peace, patience, kindness, goodness, faithfulness, gentleness, and self-control.[91] Do these sound familiar? They should! They are Jesus' resources! We shouldn't be surprised that as we root into Jesus, his Spirit will begin to shape us and then spill out of our lives.

Let's play a game for a moment. First, I'll mention a difficult scenario. Second, I'd like you to brainstorm how you might respond to each scenario **in your own power.** Go ahead, give it a try:

- **Scenario 1:** Your little brother is driving you crazy because he is lonely and wants to be around you.

- **Scenario 2:** You are tempted to look at something you know you shouldn't look at.

- **Scenario 3:** Your friend just rudely insulted you.

- **Scenario 4:** Your parents are on your case about improving your grades so you can get a good scholarship for college.

- **Scenario 5:** You are at a friend's house, and that person offers you some alcohol.

If I'm an independent, self-dependent, co-dependent person, I don't have much gentleness, patience, or self-control. Any amount of those qualities that I have in my tank gets depleted quickly in difficult situations. In fact, I emptied all of these just yesterday when I was driving in traffic!

Now, revisit those scenarios and brainstorm the type of fruit that can overflow from you as a person **rooted in Jesus**.

Jesus told his followers in John 15:16, *"I chose you. I appointed you to go and produce lasting fruit."* In Jesus we are changed and we become change agents. His resources overflow through us to make a lasting difference in our broken world. The very things in short supply in our world are produced within us when we live a rooted faith.

SEEDS

A rooted life also produces seeds. It's what healthy trees do. When we **grow down** into Jesus, God involves us in his ongoing plan to help more people root into him. Disciples make disciples who make disciples for the rest of time. *For you have been born again, but not to a life that will quickly end. Your new life will last forever because it comes from the eternal, living word of God (1 Peter 1:23).*

As Matthew 28:18-20 reveals, we are a part of God's pattern to make disciples of all nations, baptizing people in the name of the Father and of the Son and of the Holy Spirit, and teaching them to obey everything Jesus commanded. As we do this, we are assured that Jesus is with us. From his resources we're empowered to **go out** among our friends, families, communities, countries, and continents. If we aren't sure what to say to someone, the Spirit produces the words in us. Much like what happened to me on that bench outside of Starbucks (look back at Chapter 9 if you've forgotten the story), dependence on God's Spirit leads us in God's direction and enables us to sow seeds.[92]

OXYGEN

A rooted life produces life-giving oxygen. God created humanity through his words and gave us life with his breath so that we could have relationship with him.[93] But sin has ravaged humanity's ability to keep breathing. The world is suffocating and desperately needs the life of Jesus. So when Jesus commissioned his disciples to change the world, *he* **breathed** *on them and said, "Receive the Holy Spirit."*[94]

There is a wild demonstration of the breathing power of God's life-giving Spirit in the Old Testament. It's interesting to note that the Old Testament Hebrew word for *Spirit—Ruach—*can also be translated as *Breath.* So when the prophet Ezekiel had a vision of a valley strewn with skeletons, he was about to be astonished by the power of life in the Breath of God.

> "Could these bones live?" the Lord asked Ezekiel. Stunned, he responded, "Lord, only you know." So God told Ezekiel to speak to the bones: "Dry bones, listen to word of the Lord: *'I will put breath in you, and you will come to life. Then you will know that I am the Lord.'"* After speaking out, Ezekiel watched in amazement as the bones rattled, tendons and flesh

and skin grew on the bones. Then the Lord's breath entered them and they stood fully alive.[95]

The Spirit of God, the very Breath of God that gives life, is in you.

REFUGE

A rooted life produces refuge. When I asked my son how he would explain a refuge, he said that a refuge is "a place where you feel safer than the place you came from. It's a place you can call home." I agree.

Our world is scattered with refugees who need us to be a source of God's care and protection. The sin in this world has displaced many people who need a home, a secure footing, and a sanctuary. The good news is that the Jesus-centered life is like a tree that becomes a place for people to gather, to picnic, to shelter, to find shade, to pause for rest. That's what God offers:

- *The Lord is a **shelter** for the oppressed, **a refuge** in times of trouble (Psalm 9:9, bold added).*

- *The Lord is my rock, my fortress and my deliverer; my*

*God is my rock, in who I take **refuge**, my shield and the horn of my salvation, my stronghold (Psalm 18:2 NIV, bold added).*

- *Taste and see that the Lord is good. Oh, the joys of those who take **refuge** in him! (Psalm 34:8, bold added).*

- *God is our **refuge** and strength, always ready to help in times of trouble (Psalm 46:1, bold added).*

- *For you are my safe **refuge**, a fortress where my enemies cannot reach me (Psalm 61:3, bold added).*

Romans 11:16 says this: *For if the roots of the tree are holy, the branches will be, too.* And so, as we are in Christ, that's what we provide for the world, too. Psalm 104:16-17 compares God's work in us this way:

> *The trees of the Lord are well cared for—the*
> *cedars of Lebanon that he planted.*
> *There the birds make their nests, and the*
> *storks make their homes in the cypresses.*

So don't get caught fruitless! Paul says this to another vibrant group of new followers of Christ, in Philippians 1:9-11:

I pray that your love will overflow more and more, and that you will keep on growing in knowledge and understanding.... May you always be filled with the fruit of your salvation—the righteous character produced in your life by Jesus Christ—for this will bring much glory and praise to God.

GO OUT:

- In the space below, over the image of the person, draw a tree. Try to illustrate all the components talked about in this book, including the roots, trunk, knots, winds, seeds, fruit, and so on. If you like what you've drawn, consider sharing a picture of your tree on social media. **(Spread the word: #growdown)**

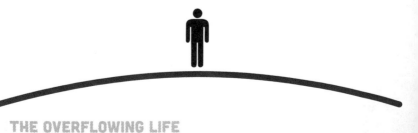

- As you look at your drawing, what fruit of the Spirit is already evident in your life? What fruit do you want and need to produce more of? What part might *you* play in seeing this happen—and how might you pray to God about *his* part?

- What can you do this week to plant the seeds of the gospel in the lives of other people?

- What difference would it make for you to live with God's breath in you?

- Have you ever known anyone who was a refuge for others? What was that person like?

- Take a moment to pray that God would let you overflow with his life.

CHAPTER 12:
SEEING THE FOREST

GROW
DOWN

Seeing the Forest *summary*

Lie down on the ground underneath a tree sometime and then look up. What would you see if you did that?

- The trunk extending upward…

- The richness of the knots beautifully ingrained into the bark…

- Countless branches shooting out in all directions from the trunk, each with a maze of other branches and twigs sprouting out, each with a blanket of numerous leaves fluttering in the breeze, each with its own fibrous network drawing up nourishment from the rooted soil.

Now picture a bundle of trees like this, maybe gathered together by a stream, as if they were having communion: the branches and leaves of this small group intertwined in a shared space; the shade they offer together more prominent; the shelter they provide for the lives of others even greater.

- Shade
- Shelter

Now picture a vast forest of trees like this, running endlessly over mountains and valleys, their entire ecosystem rich with fresh air, teeming with life, strong and vibrant in diversity, growing together.

GENERATIONAL TRANSFERENCE OF FAITH

We have a tendency in our adulterated faith to treat faith like a private matter, stemming from our pursuit of independence and self-dependence, I suppose. But faith is best understood as something we share within a collective, corporate experience. *in other words*

— private/kept to self
— needed to be shared

When Paul wrote to the Colossians, he wrote to "you" plural. When he said in chapter 2, "and now just as *you* accepted Christ Jesus," he was referring to *many people*. Many people: each one **rooting down** into Christ, **drawing up** his resources, and **overflowing** with life.

We stand in faith today because one community shared faith with the next, who shared faith with the next, who shared faith with the next, and so on until through time we came to follow Jesus as our Lord, too. And now it is our turn to share the vibrancy of faith with those who follow after us. A forest flourishes upon the seed and fertilization of the older trees. For this reason, younger people ought to express thanksgiving to older people who have given faith. And older people ought to intentionally transfer faith in such a way that younger generations will be empowered to do the same. *How?*

Two crazy words used by the first Christians help us **grow
down, draw up,** and **go out:** *didache* (teaching) and
koinonia (fellowship).[96]

- **Didache.** As we are taught the truth, we're equipped to
  pass the truth to the generations that follow us. When
  passionate Christians mentor others to live Jesus-
  centered lives, the community matures in both depth
  of faith and abundance of mission.[97]

  your didachur?

- **Koinonia:** Where two or three of us[98] gather, Jesus
  is with us. We share meals, communion, and the
  teaching of truth as a network of Christ-followers.[99] We
  rejoice with those who rejoice and mourn with those
  who mourn.[100] In the midst of turmoil, our community
  offers a refuge of peace.[101] As individuals we don't act
  like we're important, but we enjoy everyone,[102] and
  even consider others as better than ourselves.[103] This
  radical sort of community makes self-absorbed people
  very uncomfortable.[104]

  - mature

NETWORK OF MISSION

The Pando "stand" in Utah consists of 106 acres of 47,000
aspen trees. Together the trees weigh an estimated 13

million pounds! That's big! But what is truly remarkable about Pando[105] is that all of the aspen trees represent one organism that's believed to be the largest in the world. Each aspen that grows is connected to the roots of other aspen trees.[106] *What is the symbolism?*

This kind of rooted network is how truly vibrant community in the church works. A powerful example of this can be seen in Romans 16. At first glance, the list of names in this chapter might seem worthless or boring. So, just like we sometimes skip over the genealogies of Jesus at Christmastime, we're tempted to stop reading Romans (if we actually ever do read it!) at the end of chapter 15. But the 16th chapter, I believe, contains the proof that the first 15 chapters are true. *Read romans 16? How does what is happening in there compare to our daily lives? contrast?*

Read this list of names from Romans 16. Remember that these were real people, with real stories (if you don't believe me, read the whole chapter so you can see what Paul says about them). If you can't pronounce a name, give it a try anyway. Someday, when they meet you face to face in heaven, perhaps you can share a laugh:

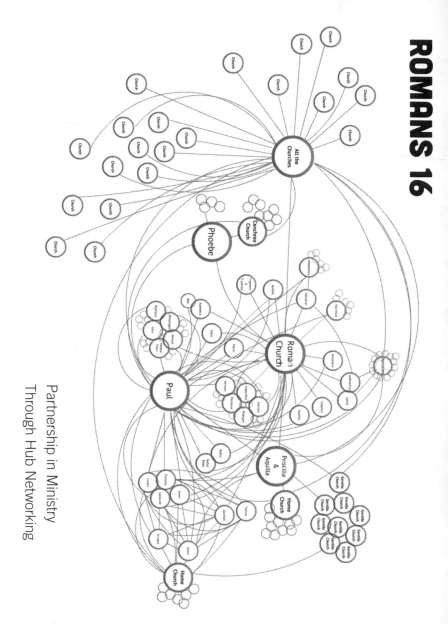

Partnership in Ministry
Through Hub Networking

- Phoebe
- Priscilla
- Aquila
- Epenetus
- Mary
- Andronicus
- Junia
- Ampliatus
- Urbanus
- Stachys
- Apelles
- Aristobulus
- Herodion
- Narcissus
- Tryphena
- Tryphosa
- Persis
- Rufus
- Rufus' mom
- Asyncritus
- Phlegon
- Hermes
- Patrobas
- Hermas
- Other brothers and sisters
- Philologus
- Julia
- Nereus
- Nereus' sister
- Olympas
- And everyone with them
- Timothy
- Lucius
- Jason
- Sosipater
- Tertius
- Gaius
- Erastus
- Quartus
- Paul

The Christian life is lived in a network with others. God built us do use our unique gifts and circumstances to encourage one another in Christ.[107] Unlike the lone-ranger mentality of adulterated faith, a life that **grows down** into Christ shares in the fellowship of those who have gone before us, are with us today, and who will be living for Jesus in the future. *We are surrounded by a huge cloud of witnesses to the life of faith.*[108]

Trees grow best within the community of other trees. Don't go it alone. Seek out a fertile community of people that is ~~intent~~ *wants* to live a Jesus-centered life, **growing down** into him, **drawing up** his resources, and **overflowing** with what he has done.

GO OUT:

- What is *didache,* and what can you do about it?

- What is *koinonia,* and what can you do about it?

- What different gifts exist within the people of your church or youth group? What unique set of gifts has God given you to help others live a Jesus-centered life?

- What do you want to be like when you're 60? What can you do now to make sure you'll be an encouraging mentor for younger people in your church network in the future?[109]

- In the diagram below, fill in the circles with names of people who are in your network of Christ-followers. Then fill in people who they also impact. Feel free to draw more networks extending from these! Take a moment to pray for the people in your network. *(Spread the word: #growdown)*

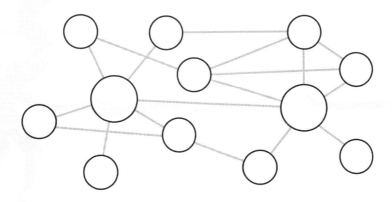

CONCLUSION:
ROOTED FAITH

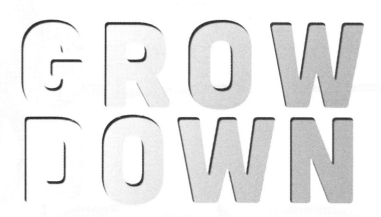

GROW DOWN

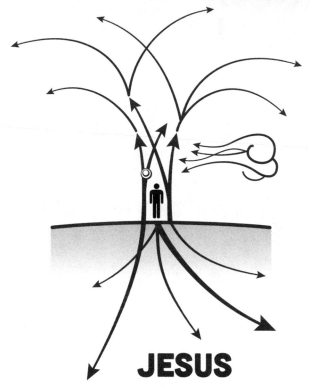

JESUS

So, what are you going to be when you *grow down*?

Here are some great answers:

- "Rooted in Christ."

- "A person who can stand through any circumstance."

- "A person who shares the life of Jesus with others."

- "Childlike in my faith."

- "An encouragement for others in my wounds."

- "Well, I won't be an adult who steps on others to get ahead in life and consumes resources just for myself. I'm going to live differently."

How would you answer this question: What are you going to be when you **grow down?** *(Spread the word: #growdown)*

As you look back at this book, which aspect of the tree impacted you most? Why?

After you put this book down, what can you do to make sure you'll be overflowing in faith?

Take a moment to rephrase Paul's prayer in Ephesians 3 and turn it into a prayer for yourself:

> *I pray that from his glorious, unlimited resources he will empower you with inner strength through his Spirit. Then Christ will make his home in your hearts as you trust in him. Your roots will grow down into God's love and keep you strong. And may you have the power to understand, as all God's people should, how wide, how long, how high, and how deep his love is. May you experience the love of Christ, though it is too great to understand fully. Then you will be made complete with all the fullness of life and power that comes from God. Now all glory to God, who is able, through his mighty power at work within us, to accomplish infinitely more than we might ask or think. Glory to him in the church and in Christ Jesus through all generations forever and ever! Amen.*[110]

ENDNOTES

[1] urbandictionary.com/define.php?term=adult

[2] "Tell him about the Twinkie" from the movie *Ghostbusters* is perhaps the most profound cultural Twinkie reference. I'm trying to come in a close second here.

[3] science.howstuffworks.com/innovation/edible-innovations/twinkie.htm (This is also the source for the quote about Twinkies as the "icon of junk food snacks.)

[4] Maybe I can illustrate this with a simple vocabulary quiz. Checkmark the following words once you understand their meaning:

- An *ad*vertisement moves you toward buying a product.

- An *ad*venture moves you toward an exciting journey.

- An *ad*versary tries to move you toward the grave!

– An *ad*aption moves you toward making something fit better (e.g. "I made an adaption in my waistline so that I could put my pants on.").

– An *ad*hesive moves you toward sticking to something (e.g. "I wish my brain was adhesive to math.").

– An *ad*viser moves you toward wisdom (hopefully).

– An *ad*orer is someone who moves you toward getting a restraining order because they won't stop creeping on you.

– An *ad*diction moves you toward something over and over again.

[5] merriam-webster.com/dictionary/adult

[6] Unfortunately, in our adulterated society it's becoming more common for children to be exposed to explicit sexual material through Internet or mobile pornography, or other more or less hideous means, at earlier ages.

[7] merriam-webster.com/dictionary/childish

[8] *Alter* is where we get words like "alteration" or "alternative."

[9] merriam-webster.com/dictionary/adulterate

[10] merriam-webster.com/dictionary/ adultery

[11] Over time, the "a" in *all* became synonymous with the "u" in *adult* because people understood that the words were inseparably linked.

[12] Marshall MacLuhan, *The Medium is the Message* (Berkeley, CA: Jerome Agel, Gingko Press, 1967, renewed 1996), 18.

[13] A.W. Tozer, *The Pursuit of God: The Human Thirst for the Divine* (Harrisburg, PA: Christian Publications, 1948), 90-94. "Like an eye which sees everything in front of it and never sees itself," Tozer wrote, "faith is occupied with the Object upon which it rests and pays no attention to itself at all. While we are looking at God we do not see ourselves – blessed riddance...[but] sin has twisted our vision inward and made it self-regarding." (Tozer, 91.)

[14] "The historical sociological markers assigning adult status – leaving home, finishing school, becoming financially independent, marriage, and child rearing– no longer become the defining characteristics of adulthood. Rather, the more subjective criteria of 'becoming independent,' 'making my own decisions,' and 'supporting myself financially' now constitute the rites of passage into adulthood." Setran David and Chris Kiesling, *Spiritual Formation in Emerging Adulthood: A Practical Theology for College and Young Adult Ministry* (Ada, MI: Baker, 2013), 59— referencing to Jeffrey Arnett, *Emerging Adulthood: The Winding Road from the Late Teens through the Twenties* (New York, NY: Oxford University Press, 2004).

[15] See Deuteronomy 5:1, 6:3-4; 2 Kings 20:16; Jeremiah 7:2; Ezekiel 6:3, 12:2, 13:2; 25:3; 37:4; Amos 7:6; Micah 6:2; Zechariah 8:9; Matthew 11:15, 13:9,43; Mark 4:9,20,23-24; 8:18; Luke 8:8-21; 11:28; 14:35; John 5:25,28; 8:47; 9:27; Acts 13:44; Romans 11:8; Hebrews 3:7,15; Revelation 2:7,11,17,29; 3:6,13,22; 13:9. (Those who obey God's word will produce an abundance of life. Mark 4:20; Lk 8:15. Those who listen to God belong to God. John 5:47.)

[16] Matthew 13:9-17

[17] "Unbelief has put us perilously close to the sin of Lucifer who said, 'I will set my throne above the throne of God.'" Tozer, *The Pursuit of God,* 85.

[18] See Chapter 1 of Tozer's book *The Pursuit of God* for more discussion on how sin has tricked us into a desire to "possess, always possess."

[19] Adults have become blind to the plank in their own eye. Research has shown that "most problems and issues that adults typically consider teenage problems are in fact closely linked to adult-world problems." Christian Smith and Melinda Denton *Soul Searching: The Religious and Spiritual Lives of American Teenagers* (New York, NY: Oxford, 2005), 271.

[20] If the Apostle Paul were here, he would yell: "What magician has deceived you? You once believed in Jesus, but you have added other things to your lives. God's real children are those who put their faith in God. Have you lost your senses?" (See Galatians 3:1-7.)

[21] Del Griffith, played by John Candy, and Neal Page, played by Steve Martin

[22] Don't worry; after scraping their car between two semi-trucks, the two survive and eventually make it home—but not until they learn some valuable lessons about depending on one another.

[23] See 1 Corinthians 13:11; 14:20

[24] Tozer, *The Pursuit of God,* 18.

[25] See Matthew 18:1-9

[26] The simple fact that they couldn't figure out the answer and had to ask Jesus which of them was the greatest proved their limited abilities.

[27] Notice Jesus' own example in this. He didn't join the argument, claiming to be the greatest himself (even though he was!).

[28] See also Matthew 19:13-15 and Mark 10:13-16

[29] Colossians 1:17

[30] Colossians 2:13-14

ENDNOTES

[31] My middle name is "Chapman," after a great-great-great-great-grandmother of mine who may have been his sister—but don't tell anyone.

[32] See Colossians 3:4

[33] See Colossians 1:22-23; "The Christian's identity and value do not reside in the fragile order and tenuous control that she or he imposes upon life. Identity and value are found in a vital and living relationship with Christ our Lord. This relationship liberates Christians from dependence upon their little systems of order and fragile structures of control." M. Robert Mulholland Jr., *Invitation to a Journey: A Road Map for Spiritual Formation* (Westmont, IL: IVP, 1993), 89.

[34] Colossians 3:17

[35] See Colossians 3:5-9

[36] Colossians 1:9–4:13

[37] Tozer, *The Pursuit of God*, 85.

[38] See Colossians 1:5-6, 23

[39] See Colossians 3:18–4:1; 4:9; Philemon 1

[40] See Colossians 1:24; 2:5,19; 4:2-6

[41] See Genesis 18:1-15

[42] See Exodus 3:1–4:31

[43] See Matthew 23:1-36

[44] See John 21:15-19

[45] See Acts 9:1-8

[46] See Numbers 13:25–14:12

[47] See 1 Samuel 3:1-14

[48] See Matthew 1:18; Luke 1:26-56; 2:1-7

[49] Luke 18:27

[50] See 2 Samuel 12; Psalm 51

[51] Talk with your youth pastor or small-group leader, or with other teenagers who are truly leading a Jesus-centered life. They will likely have suggestions on great resources.

[52] Psalm 1:1-3 (NIV), bold added

[53] Though in Jesus I am a mighty man! The weak are made strong, and the short are made tall—or something like that.

[54] See Romans 3:23

[55] See Colossians 1:15-20

[56] The Message translation presents part of this passage like this: *From beginning to end he's there, towering far above everything, everyone. So spacious is he, so roomy, that everything of God finds its proper place in him without crowding. Colossians 1:18-20 (The Message).*

[57] Anselm of Canterbury: *The Major Works* (New York, NY: Oxford University Press, 2008), 87, quoting Anselm's *Proslogion*, chapter II.

[58] See Colossians 1:20

[59] That is, if there is "sleep" and if there are "days" in heaven. No matter what, it's going to be good.

[60] None of us could think up everything. So here are some examples of Jesus' unlimited resources (with some Bible verses to look up sometime): Love, Joy, Peace, Patience, Kindness, Goodness, Faithfulness, Gentleness, Self-Control, Mercy, Knowledge, Justice, Holiness, Goodness, Majesty, Redemption. And here are some more with some Bible references attached:

- Eternal life (John 3:14-16,36; 5:24-25; 6:40; Romans 6:23)

- All authority (Matthew 28:18; John 13:1; Ephesians 1:21)

- Salvation (Psalm 121; Isaiah 25:9; 45:17; Joel 2:32; Mark 16:16; John 10:9; Acts 4:12)

- Assurance (Colossians 1:27; 1 Thessalonians 1:5; Hebrews 10:39)

- Grace (John 1:17; Romans 1:7; 3:24; 5:15; 2 Corinthians 12:9; Ephesians 2:5)

- Comfort (Psalm 23:4; Isaiah 40:1; Matthew 5:4)

- Creativity (Genesis 1; Isaiah 40:28; Romans 1:25; Ephesians 2:10; 3:9, 14; Colossians 1:15-17)

– Endurance (Psalm 106:1; Revelation 1:9)

– Forgiveness (Isaiah 53:4-6; Matthew 6:12; 26:28; Romans 5:15-19; Galatians 1:4; 1 John 1:9)

– Healing (Genesis 20:17; Psalm 30:2; Isaiah 53:5; 61:1; Mark 1:30-34; 1 Peter 2:24)

– Guidance (Psalm 23:1-4; 119:105; 1 Peter 5:4)

– Holiness (1 Chronicles 16:29; Psalm 29:2; 96:9; Matthew 5:48; Luke 4:34)

[61] See John 10:28

[62] See Acts 17:28

[63] Matthew 7:24-27

[64] Eugene Peterson, *Answering God: The Psalms as Tools for Prayer* (New York, NY: HarperOne; reprint edition, 1991), 27.

[65] See Psalm 145:18

[66] 1 Timothy 4:12

[67] Francis Chan, *Multiply: Disciples Making Disciples* (Colorado Springs, CO: David C. Cook, 2012), 270.

[68] emeraldashborer.info/index.cfm#sthash. DweDfDPA.dpbs

[69] Colossians 1:22-23

[70] See Colossians 2:8-9

[71] See Colossians 2:10

[72] Name and details omitted to protect the people involved in this story.

[73] See Isaiah 52:13–53:12; Luke 24:38-39; John 20:24-29

[74] Romans 10:15 (quoting Isaiah 52:7)

[75] The song is found on the band's album of the same name, *Beautiful Things,* released in 2010 by Brash Music.

[76] Acts 4:20

[77] Colossians 1:4

[78] Chan, *Multiply*, 291.

[79] Only 28 percent of congregations characterized themselves as having a "high spiritual vitality" in 2010, down from 43 percent in 2005. Thom and Joani Schultz, *Why Nobody Wants to Go to Church Anymore: And How 4 Acts of Love Will Make Your Church Irresistible* (Loveland, CO: Group, 2013), 13.

[80] Ibid.,13.

[81] Ibid., 17.

[82] Ibid., 18.

[83] Ibid., 13.

[84] Ibid., 18.

[85] See Matthew 13:31-32; 17:20-21

[86] Acts 1:8

[87] *"You cannot be fruitful unless you remain in me."* (John 15:4, Jesus speaking).

[88] See Mark 11:12-21

[89] At another time, in Matthew 15:13, Jesus told them, *"Every plant not planted by my heavenly Father will be uprooted."*

[90] Cursing in Scripture is reserved for the worst of sinners, especially those who pretend outwardly to be close to God but who lack the inner heart of faith to produce fruit from God. See Matthew 23:1-36; 25:31-46

[91] See Galatians 5:22-23

[92] See Luke 12:12

[93] See Genesis 2:7

[94] John 20:22, bold added

[95] Ezekiel 37

[96] See Acts 2:42-47

[97] See Ephesians 4:12; 1 John 1:3. "We are called to make disciples and strengthening the other members of the church body is an important part of this." Chan, *Multiply*, 74.

[107] See Ephesians 4:7

[108] Hebrews 12:1

[109] Thank you to Pastor Troy Bondy for asking me this question!

[110] Ephesians 3:15-21

98 See Matthew 18:20

99 See Acts 2:42

100 See Romans 12:15

101 See Colossians 3:15

102 See Romans 12:16

103 See Philippians 2:3

104 "He calls each one he meets into a personal, intimate relationship with himself. But as he invites people to follow him, he is also telling them that they must make a choice. If they choose one thing, it means refusing another. If they choose to follow Jesus, they receive a gift of love and communion, but at the same time they must say 'no' to the ways of the world and accept loss; they must own their choice." Jean Vanier, *From Brokenness to Community* (Mahwah, NJ: Paulist Press, 1992), 10.

105 *Pando* is a Latin word meaning "to spread."

106 pagosa.com/adventureguide/observing-colorado-aspen-largest-living-earth/